Hot PROPERTY: The SCOTT BROTHERS Coloring Book

Alex Silver

(c) 2017 Alex Silver

All rights reserved.

ISBN-13: 978-1-945887-42-0

ISBN-10: 1-945887-42-7

Every effort has been made to ensure that the information in this book was correct at press time. The author and publisher disclaim liability to any party for any loss, damage, or disruption caused by errors or omissions, whether such errors or omissions result from negligence, accident, or any other cause.

Visit us at gumdroppress.com

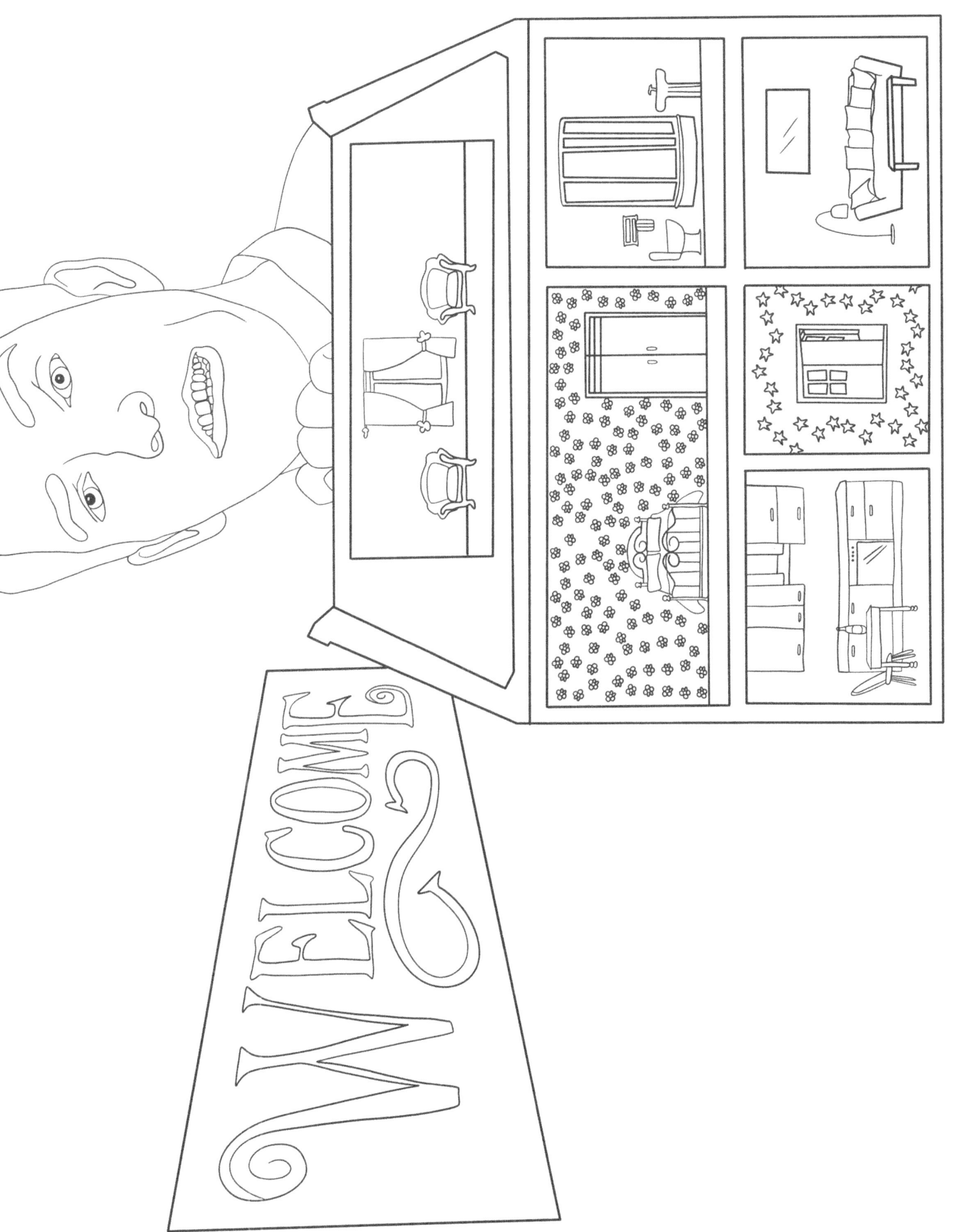